how2become.com

RAPID STUDY SKILLS FOR STUDENTS:
ESSENTIAL WRITING TIPS POCKETBOOK

www.How2Become.com

Orders: Please contact How2Become Ltd, Suite 3, 40 Churchill Square Business Centre, Kings Hill, Kent ME19 4YU.

You can order through Amazon.co.uk under ISBN 9781911259909, via the website www.How2Become.com, Gardners or Bertrams.

ISBN: 9781911259909

First published in 2017 by How2Become Ltd.

Updated in 2018.

Typeset for How2Become Ltd by Gemma Butler.

Disclaimer

Every effort has been made to ensure that the information contained within this guide is accurate at the time of publication. How2Become Ltd is not responsible for anyone failing any part of any selection process as a result of the information contained within this guide. How2Become Ltd and their authors cannot accept any responsibility for any errors or omissions within this guide, however caused. No responsibility for loss or damage occasioned by any person acting, or refraining from action, as a result of the material in this publication can be accepted by How2Become Ltd.

The information within this guide does not represent the views of any third-party service or organisation.

CONTENTS

INTRODUCTION

WHY READ THIS BOOK?

No matter which stage of academia you are at, writing to a high standard is extremely important. It is the mode by which you transmit your ideas, findings, opinions, critiques, and knowledge. So, it is vital that you are always looking to improve upon your writing skills.

In exam and essay situations, clear written communication is as important as anything else. As you have probably seen, students with better ideas often do not get more marks than students with superior writing skills; you cannot get high marks in an essay off the back of good ideas alone.

This book can become your go-to resource when you've got your killer idea, but need that little nudge to express it in the way it deserves: concisely and accurately. You may not need to read it cover-to-cover; look through the contents and dip into the sections relevant to you.

So, onwards to the first section: punctuation.

PUNCTUATION

In English, punctuation consists of a number of symbols, marks, or signs which are deployed around letters and words, in order to convey the writer's intended meaning. The use of spacing also comes under punctuation. All the different punctuation marks perform different jobs within a sentence, all of which are important.

Punctuation is a good place to start when discussing writing, as it allows us to give meaning and form to our words and sentences. Without punctuation, comprehending writing of any length would be nigh on impossible. This is the point of punctuation – to aid understanding. **It is NOT used to show where the reader should pause or 'breathe'.**

Another reason to begin by looking at punctuation is because its rules are mostly set in stone. For academic writing, personal style should not affect how you use punctuation – at least not too much. Each punctuation mark has its own specific use, which helps to convey a specific meaning within a sentence.

So, using different punctuation marks in different places within the same sentence will alter its meaning.

For example:

A woman, without her man, is nothing.

A woman: without her, man is nothing.

THE FULL STOP (.)

Of course, the main use of a full stop is to show where a sentence ends. The examples below are all 'complete' sentences, which are what you should be writing in. For example:

While this is simple, let's look now at what constitutes a complete sentence.

A complete sentence will always contain at least one main clause. A main clause will contain a subject as well as a verb to act on this subject.

Have another look at the example sentences used above. This time, you will find the subjects of the sentences highlighted, and the verbs of the sentences underlined.

- *American writer* Mark Twain *was born* *in Missouri.*

- *The tallest mountain in Ecuador <u>is called</u> 'Chimborazo'.*

- *The sale of vehicles <u>represents</u> the United Kingdom's second-largest export.*

If you are unsure as to whether a sentence you have written is incomplete, try to identify its subject(s) and verb(s). If you can't, you may not have written a complete sentence – you may have written a sentence fragment.

Examples of Sentence Fragments

Riding on the coattails of another's successes.

To visit her friend on St. Patrick's Day.

And went to Dudley for work experience.

As you can see, the above 'sentences' do not show verbs acting on subjects – their subjects are implied. In the first one, we do not know *who* has been riding on the coattails. Therefore, the phrase is merely a sentence fragment. As a general rule, you should avoid using sentence fragments in your writing.

THE COMMA (,)

The comma is a deceptively difficult piece of punctuation to use. For this reason, it is often misused and/or overused. The difficulty lies in the fact that there are many different writing situations that require the use of a comma, and many situations where its use would be incorrect.

So, we can say that there are many different types of comma.

The simplest use of the comma is to separate nouns in a list.

For example:

The government is prioritising education, health, and libraries.

The new signing brings pace, power, and vision to the squad.

Bleak House, *Great Expectations*, and *Little Dorrit* are all works by Charles Dickens.

Note: The examples given above all employ the 'Oxford Comma' or 'serial comma' (a comma between the penultimate item in the list and 'and'), which is generally seen as being optional.

THE OXFORD COMMA

Those in favour of the Oxford comma suggest it can bring clarity to certain situations. For example, consider the following two versions of this sentence:

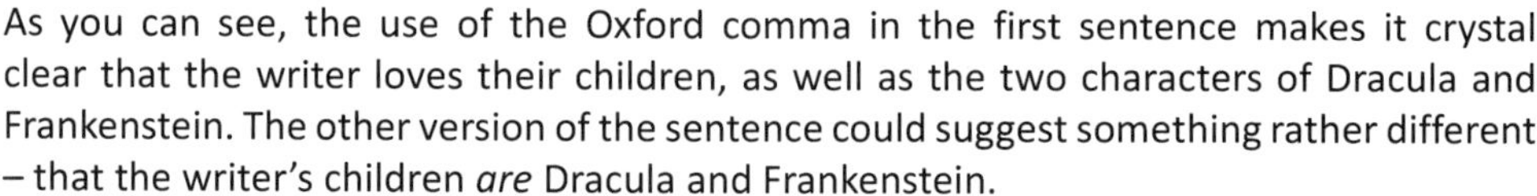

- 'I love my children, Dracula, and Frankenstein.'

- 'I love my children, Dracula and Frankenstein.'

As you can see, the use of the Oxford comma in the first sentence makes it crystal clear that the writer loves their children, as well as the two characters of Dracula and Frankenstein. The other version of the sentence could suggest something rather different – that the writer's children *are* Dracula and Frankenstein.

As when listing nouns, commas are also used to separate listed adjectives and adverbs. Think about when you want to describe something with more than one word in a row. You'd use commas to separate these words!

For example:

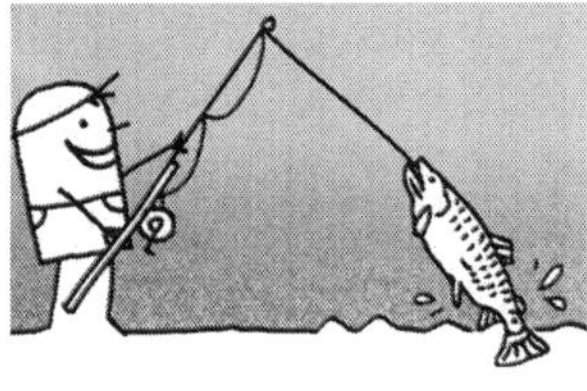

The great, grey mountain peak stood ominously above the village.

Move the rod slowly, precisely, and decisively if you want to catch a fish.

The lavender plant is known for its fragrant, colourful, and attractive flowers.

Another extremely common use of the comma is to separate clauses within sentences.

For example:

Ricardo bought a new pair of shoes, but did not get his watch repaired as intended.

As the room filled with water, the family became more and more afraid.

I've never watched musicals, and don't intend to start doing so now.

While this type of comma is the most frequently used, make sure you use it correctly. In other words, beware the comma splice.

THE COMMA SPLICE

A comma splice occurs when a writer employs a comma to link two independent clauses – clauses that could make sense on their own as sentences. As shown above, a comma can be used to separate such clauses within one sentence, but with the use of other connective words like 'and' or 'but'. So, when a comma is used to separate two independent clauses (clauses that could make sense on their own as sentences), an error occurs.

For example (these are INCORRECT sample sentences):

A lioness's top speed is around 50mph, they can run fast in short bursts.

I enjoy playing the piano, I use it to relax.

The Battle of Maidstone took place in June 1648, it ended in victory for the parliamentarians.

The problem with these sentences is that a comma is not sufficient to link them. The two clauses either need to be in their own sentences, or connectives/a different punctuation mark needs to be used. See below for correct versions of the three wrong examples given above. The highlighted areas show what has been changed to make the sentences correct.

A lioness's top speed is around 50mph; they can run fast in short bursts.

I enjoy playing the piano. I use it to relax.

The Battle of Maidstone took place in June 1648, and it ended in victory for the parliamentarians.

Similarly, commas are also used to separate introductory parts of a sentence from its main clause.

For example:

After arriving home from the festival, Nathan fired up his computer.

Despite initial disagreement, the deal was struck relatively quickly.

Fortunately, there was not too much damage.

A further use of the comma is to separate 'extra' details of a sentence from its main clause. In these cases, two commas would be used to contain the 'extra' information from the main content of the sentence. A good way to check if you are using this type of comma correctly is to take out the 'extra' information and see if the main clause makes sense by itself. If it does, you're looking good.

For example:

The beach, which was empty and serene, was her favourite place to spend time.

Seoul's Olympic Park, which played host to the 1988 Olympics, was renovated in 2011.

Rahul, my cousin, graduated from university this summer.

Commas also have an important role to play when writing dialogue or direct speech. Namely, they are used to separate the direct speech from the rest of the sentence.

For example:

Note: The rules surrounding comma splices and direct speech are murky at best. In many situations, such as when writing novels, a comma splice as we've discussed is often not seen as a mistake — more of a stylistic choice. (see the second example above.) In academic writing, should it be relevant, it's probably best to err on the side of caution. Perhaps ask a teacher, tutor, or advisor about their preference on the matter!

THE COLON (:)

While the comma is deceptively difficult to use, the colon is deceptively easy. That is to say, its uses are relatively few and clear.

Firstly, its most simple use is to introduce listed nouns.

For example:

The ingredients are simple: milk, eggs, flour, and butter.

There were myriad treasures underneath: precious stones, jewellery, coins, everything.

She wrote down what was most important to her: her dog, her friends, and work.

Note: when using colons in this way, you should make sure that the introductory part of the sentence would make sense on its own. For example, you should NOT write – 'The ingredients are: milk, eggs, flower, and butter.' You would not need to use a colon in this case. So, the colon is not <u>required</u> for every situation to do with introducing lists, although it can add clarity and style.

Another prominent use of the colon is to reveal and develop themes and ideas within a sentence. While this sounds complicated, you'll see from the examples that it's actually quite simple.

For example:

This is most often done for emphasis.

Again, the part of the sentence that falls before the colon should make sense on its own. However, in creative writing, you may wish to flout this rule should it muscle in on your style too much.

THE SEMICOLON (;)

The semicolon is probably the most complained-about punctuation mark. Be it confused novices struggling to get to grips with it, or smug veterans maligning its misuse, you'll have heard people arguing about the semicolon.

In truth, it's not that interesting, or even that difficult to use.

Its main use is to separate two independent clauses that are closely related. This means that the two halves of the sentence must be able to make sense by themselves. In other words, your sentence containing the semicolon could feasibly be split into two perfect sentences.

However, the choice not to split them in this way, and instead employ a semicolon, would be a choice to emphasise a link of some sort between the two clauses.

For example:

Think back to the section about the comma splice – the semicolon could stand in for an erroneous comma in these situations.

Also, make sure that you are not using a semicolon where a colon would be more appropriate. In many situations, if what follows your semicolon could not make sense as its own sentence, a colon would be more appropriate.

However, in cases like this, it may be preferable to rewrite your sentence into two sentences, or use a comma and a connective!

For example:

INCORRECT:	In 1982, Mexico suffered a terrible tragedy; the eruption of El Chichón.
CORRECT:	In 1982, Mexico suffered a terrible tragedy: the eruption of El Chichón.
CORRECT:	In 1982, Mexico suffered a terrible tragedy. It was the eruption of El Chichón.

Note: see how 'It was' was added to the second part of the third example to create a second complete sentence.

Another use of the semicolon is to separate items in a list which are long or convoluted in some way. This is done to provide clarity and understanding where simply using commas would not have been sufficient.

For example:

Belligerents of the War of the Roses included: Henry VI, House of Lancaster; Henry VII, House of Tudor; Margaret of Anjou, House of Valois-Anjou; and Edward IV, House of York.

As you can see, using semicolons to separate the listed items here allows the use of the comma within the listed items themselves, and makes it clear the Houses belong with the respective rulers. It even has the use of an Oxford semicolon...

So, let's look at what this list would have looked like without the use of the semicolon:

For example (this is an INCORRECT sample sentence):

Belligerents of the War of the Roses included: Henry VI, House of Lancaster, Henry VII, House of Tudor, Margaret of Anjou, House of Valois-Anjou, and Edward IV, House of York.

This sentence is much more confusing; the reader has been led to believe that the Houses are separate from the rulers. The semicolon is the saviour of this situation.

THE HYPHEN (–)

The hyphen (-) is another potentially tricky piece of punctuation to use correctly. It is often confused with the dash (–), its longer cousin. We'll cover the dash in the next section.

Despite potential hurdles, the hyphen has a clear set of rules surrounding its use. However, it can get complicated. Let's look at a few examples.

Hyphens are most often used within adjectives that are made up of two (or more) words and other compound words.

For example:

Twenty-first century literature.

An off-the-cuff remark.

A self-diagnosed illness.

However, it is easy to make mistakes and use hyphens when there is no need to. For example, if you wanted to use 'off the cuff' adverbially rather than as an adjective (describing a verb rather than a noun), then you should not use hyphens.

For example:

The remark was made off the cuff.

Also, hyphens should not be employed in sentences where these types of adjectives follow the noun. In the first three examples above, they precede the noun.

For example:

The remark was off the cuff.

The century was the twenty first.

The illness was self-diagnosed.   (*This is an exception! See below.*)

However, in a quirk of the language, the same is not true of compound words containing the word 'self', such as 'self-diagnosed'. When using this word following a noun, the hyphen stays.

For example:

The illness was self-diagnosed.

They considered themselves to be quite self-sufficient.

The archetypal villain is ruthless and self-serving.

THE DASH (–)

The dash, often confused with the hyphen, is a completely different punctuation mark to its shorter counterpart. It serves an entirely different purpose within a sentence, and is in no way interchangeable!

In Creative Writing, the main use of the dash is to signal an 'interruption' within a sentence. This could be in the shape of a change of subject, theme, or tone. When writing dialogue, even, this could be a literal interruption!

However, in academic writing, the use of the dash would be a stylistic choice to represent a change of direction within a sentence, or to provide juxtaposition between two clauses in a sentence. Overall though, it's probably good advice to use the dash sparingly. See below for some examples of its use.

For example:

Edgar was set to become Earl of Gloucester and inherit his father's title – but Edmund had other ideas.

Rules are rules, of course – yet they are made to be broken.

She was shy, quiet, and unassuming – or so she'd have you believe.

Another way the dash is used is similar to how commas that separate 'extra information' from main clauses of sentences are used. So, in these situations, you'd need to use a pair of dashes.

For example:

The beach – which was empty and serene – was her favourite place to spend time.

Seoul's Olympic Park – which played host to the 1988 Olympics – was renovated in 2011.

Rahul – my cousin – graduated from university this summer.

While this usage of the dash seems interchangeable with the commas mentioned above, they convey a slightly different meaning or connotation. Namely, the choice to use dashes instead of commas in a situation like this would be the choice to write a more emphatic sentence.

In other words, if the 'extra information' you wish to include within your sentence is more important, or you wish to draw more attention to it, perhaps you'd prefer the use of dashes (over commas) to contain it. In creative writing, this is certainly something to experiment with. When writing dialogue, for example, a pair of dashes could be used when you wish your character to go off track in the middle of a sentence before resuming.

For example:

"*I'm very angry with you – I'll deal with Maurice later – you're in so much trouble.*"

"*Mrs. Haverley is fully booked all week – I need to tell Mason, actually – please don't bother her.*"

"*As you can see, the River Nile stretches from – Jeff, stop talking – all the way down in Uganda, through the continent, and up into the Mediterranean Sea.*"

However, in most situations, you should stick to using commas to separate extra information like this in a sentence. The use of dashes in this way could even be considered incorrect if the extra information does not represent a clear enough interruption of the sentence.

CRAFTING SENTENCES

Now that we've shown you how to craft a sentence, let's dive into what makes a 'good sentence', and what you should be aiming for when writing under formal conditions.

A good starting point would be to think about the length of your sentences. In many cases, you should aim to keep your sentences as short as possible. This is not for word count-related reasons, but to keep your sentences concise and focused. Essentially, it ensures you are not writing 'empty' sentences or waffling.

Of course, in creative writing, such a hard-and-fast rule could stymie your voice or stifle a particular mood that you were aiming to create. In these cases, don't let ruthless efficiency get in the way of your style.

So, let's have a look at how you can cut the excess words from your sentences.

For example:

> Without question, it is possible to say that the Fool has an important role to play in the plot of King Lear. This character represents Lear's conscience throughout and, ironically, acts a foil to his foolishness.

This could become:

> The Fool represents Lear's conscience throughout and, ironically, acts as a foil to his foolishness.

Avoiding repetition is an effective way to sharpen up a sentence; you don't need to say the same thing in many different ways. If you are writing an essay, repetition will not further your point or improve your work. It could even cause whoever's marking to lose interest or penalise you. You don't want to create the impression that you're fluffing up your writing to meet the word count – quite the opposite.

Make your reader feel as if every word was selected for a clear and proactive reason. If you're looking to cut down a piece of writing that's over the word limit, experiment with taking out words and phrases that could be considered as overkill. A lot of the time, you'll find that the meaning of what you're saying hasn't changed, and your writing has become punchier and more impactful.

CREATING PARAGRAPHS

In this section, we're going to look beyond creating sentences and look at how best to weave them together to craft paragraphs. Luckily, in academic or any sort of formal writing, there are clear rules you can follow to make sure that your paragraphs are concise, focused, and driving your point forwards. Read on for our tips on creating paragraphs.

PARAGRAPH STRUCTURE

In academic writing or essay writing, it is extremely important to write good paragraphs. A good paragraph is one that is contained, and one that does not contain lots of complex points.

As a rule, you should try and keep paragraphs limited to one main point. This way, you can stop paragraphs from growing out of control, allowing the reader to understand your argument more easily.

A great way to make your paragraphs easier to follow is to treat each of them as a miniature essay. By this, we mean that each paragraph should have a short sentence which introduces the main point, followed by the point itself. Finally, you should end the paragraph with a short sentence which briefly summarises your point, and demonstrates how it relates to the question that you're answering. This way, you'll have your argument for each paragraph clearly laid out for the reader to see.

If it helps, you can try coming up with a subtitle for each paragraph in your essay. Don't include this in the finished copy, but writing each paragraph with the main point of it explicitly in mind will help you focus your efforts, and create a more consistent piece of work.

Once you have a paragraph structure laid out, the flow of your essay will become a lot more pronounced. This means that you'll be able to spot parts that feel disjointed and correct their course. By 'disjointed', we mean parts of the essay which either stick out from the flow of your essay and don't lead to any new points, or sections which actively move against the flow of your essay.

Imagine your essay is a river. Each part of the essay should flow into the next, as your argument cumulatively builds up towards the conclusion. The points made in earlier paragraphs should always contribute to later ones, and those which don't could be considered as irrelevant.

For example, if paragraphs A, B, C, and D all support a larger argument made in paragraph F, but the argument in paragraph E has no bearing on this argument, then you need to consider whether it's paying off for you. If the paragraph isn't benefitting your argument, then you should probably get rid of it and use the space to write something relevant.

There's no set length that a paragraph needs to be, but they can be too long. If you have a single paragraph that's significantly larger than the rest of your essay, it might be worth revisiting to see how it can be divided into smaller parts. This will prevent your essay from becoming 'bogged down'. Likewise, lots of tiny paragraphs can look too fragmented or poorly developed.

NOTE-TAKING

Before starting a written project, it's highly likely that you'll need to take notes of some description. Whether it's part of your academic research, or brainstorming plot points and character arcs for creative writing, effective note-taking should be high on your list of priorities. This is a deceptively difficult task – it's easy to write notes that may not be doing a lot for you. Let's look at some techniques you can employ to maximise the quality of your notes, while minimising the amount of time spent on them.

1. Keep your notes simple.

- Try to boil down your thoughts into key words and phrases.

- This will make your notes easier to revise and remember.

- Shorter, more focused notes, will help you to structure your ideas.

2. Know what you want to say.

> Although note-taking could help you decide on the direction of your essay or other piece of work, it's best to go into it with clear objectives. Know what you're aiming to get out of your notes, and be selective with what you actually highlight/jot down. If it's not going to help with your specific task – don't waste time noting it down!

3. Develop your notes.

- Over time, you'll want your notes to gradually become more advanced – up until the point when you'll transform them into a detailed plan.

- Spider diagrams are a good place to start. These are useful for collecting your ideas all on one page. You can also show connections between points with drawn lines and colours.

- Then, you can flesh out these points into linear notes. Here you can organise using headings and sub-headings, and underline what's most important.

Following this stage, you'll have the basis of a detailed plan – the natural next step!

DON'T FORGET TO MIND THE GAP

Sadly, this doesn't involve an exciting trip to London; it's a simple acronym you can use to keep your note-taking focused. It's particularly relevant for creative writing, and should serve to guide any research you're carrying out in preparation for embarking on your project.

Genre – When taking notes before your project, know the conventions of the genre you are aiming to write within. For example, if you are writing a horror novel, you might read and make notes from a number of horror works to ascertain what makes them fit the bill. Is it the use of characters, setting, or plot? There won't be one clear answer, but focused note-taking in this way will help you to no end when writing.

Audience – Again, it is important to be mindful of who you expect to get the most out of your writing. For example, if you are aiming to write a novel that resonates with people in their 20s, you'll want to research and take notes on novels which have successfully done this. How have the writers tailored their work to their specific audience? Perhaps there is no cut-and-dry answer, but you might be surprised at the similarities between writing aimed at the same demographics.

Purpose – Similarly, during your research stages, you need to have a clear view of what you're hoping to achieve with your work. Again, this is how you will be able to carry out productive and relevant note-taking. Once you know this, you can examine works which have achieved the same or similar effects. Thorough analysis like this will pay off – knowledge of *how* great writers do what they do will show in your work.

ESSAY WRITING

Now that we've covered more general writing tips about sentences, paragraphs, and style, let's focus on the practicalities of what it's all about as a student: essay writing. Whether you are at school or university, you'll have to spend a lot of time planning, writing, and proofreading assessed work. If this sounds like a nightmare to you, then here's ten top tips on getting an amazing mark on your next essay!

1. Read the question carefully and make sure that you understand it.

There's only one thing worse than realising you've misunderstood a question halfway through writing your essay, and that's realising you've misunderstood it *after* you get your marks back. Some people like to jump into an essay as soon as they've found a question that they think is interesting. However, by being too eager, students can end up either making more work for themselves when they have to re-write their entire essay, or lose marks because they didn't fully understand the question.

Having a strong understanding of your essay title will help you to write the best answer possible. Pay attention to the scope of the question, and look at things such as timeframes. Additionally, make sure that you understand exactly what the question is asking of you. It's never a good idea just to throw everything you know at an essay. Think about what's relevant to the question being asked, then cater your knowledge to it.

2. Take planning seriously.

The best essays come about from meticulous research and planning. Some people spend only a little amount of time on the planning stage of their essay, leaving the bulk of the work for the writing stage. While this may work for some people, what you'll likely find is that you've forgotten something when planning and now have to find a place for it in your essay. This can result in a messy structure, and your essay can lose focus.

The best way to avoid this is to devote more time to the planning stage of your essay. Your plan should be as robust as possible, briefly detailing each section and paragraph. This way, you'll probably end up doing most of the work in the planning stage of the essay-writing process.

Once your plan is finished, and you're happy with the flow of it, then you should start writing the essay. You might find that the actual essay-writing part is easy – all you're doing is turning all of the points you've made in your plan into full-sentences and paragraphs. This also means that you can spot any problems with your essay in the earliest stage, before you've done the bulk of the actual writing. Finally, a strong essay plan will let you know where your argument is going before you've started writing, meaning you can tighten up your ideas rather than just make things up as you go along.

3. Make your essay laser-focused.

Don't *literally* write an essay on lasers. Instead, make sure that your essay is incredibly focused, since this will stop your work from trying to take on too much. Make sure you answer the question, but don't be afraid to take a narrow focus. It's almost always better to go in-depth on a small number of issues, rather than have a shallow analysis of lots of issues. At degree level, your work needs to have depth, so be willing to sacrifice breadth in order to get it.

For example, if a question requires you to use case studies to support your argument, consider looking at just one in more detail, rather than many in brief. This will also help you from going off on a tangent if you force yourself to narrow your focus.

Finally, having a very narrow focus gives you the opportunity to be original in a way that doesn't make sweeping generalisations. A very specific scope gives you the opportunity to go into detail on a minute area, which in turn might give you the chance to say something truly unique.

4. Be concise.

Flowery language and long words aren't always the most appropriate when writing an essay. Of course, you should have some kind of writing style, but this doesn't mean that you need to become incomprehensible. You should aim to make your language easy to understand, with sentence structure that doesn't spiral out of control. As a general rule, short sentences are preferable to longer ones, since you can prevent run-on sentences and a general lack of focus. The goal of an essay is to convey an argument, not to show off with fancy sentence structure. Be sensible and cut out nonsense.

5. Avoid clichés.

One of the most important things to remember when trying to get a first in your next essay is to avoid clichés. This is vital because whoever is marking your work doesn't want to be bored by the same ideas, phrases, and rhetorical devices. For instance, grand-standing is a cliché which detracts from the focus of an essay, and makes it more generic.

Here's an example of grand-standing:

*"Since the **dawn of human civilisation**, scholars have discussed what it means to be human..."*

While this might be the case, it's very unlikely that opening your essay with this phrase will be of any use to your argument. It doesn't shine any light on what you're going to say – all it does is waste space, which could be spent on meaningful discussion. Clichés like this don't come across as confident – it looks clumsy. As we mentioned previously, try and keep your argument to the point, rather than relying on rhetorical devices.

6. Paraphrasing is better than writing quotations.

Throughout your education, you might have been taught to quote from sources very frequently. While it's vital that you back up any claim that you make with evidence, a quote often isn't the best way to do so. Let's take a look at why.

When you use a quote as evidence, you'll probably be using it in the following format:

1. Introduce the point you want to make.

2. Give a quote to support the point.

3. Explain what the quote is saying.

4. Explain how this is relevant to your point, as well as the essay question.

When you explain what the quote is saying, you'll probably end up repeating some of the things that have been said. Therefore, you've wasted some space by writing the quote, then putting it in your own words. Instead, you can save space (and look more sophisticated) by ditching quotes and just paraphrasing instead. Not only does this save space, but it also proves that you understand the quote and know what you're talking about.

In some cases, however, it might still be relevant to include the full quote. For example, if you're quoting a line from a Shakespeare play, then the structure of the line, as well as the exact wording, is relevant. So, in these cases, you should opt to provide a quote in its entirety.

7. Make sure your referencing is correct and presentable.

When writing an academic essay, good referencing discipline is vital. Find out what system the relevant assessing body prefers (e.g. Harvard referencing, APA, MLA, Chicago/Turabian) and then stick to it strictly. There are plenty of referencing guides online which will show you how to reference every kind of media possible – from written journals to YouTube videos. Go through your entire essay, and make sure that you've cited all of the sources you've used properly. This is an easy way to stop yourself from dropping marks.

8. Be original.

Originality is a tricky area when it comes to writing an essay. The likelihood is that you're not going to be able to change the world in a single essay. Scholars devote their whole lives and thousands of pages to even the smallest of advances in their own fields. You've probably only got a few weeks and maybe a few thousand words.

Likewise, it probably seems as if all the big ideas have already been made. If you find yourself coming up with a radically new idea when writing an essay, the chances are that someone has already written about it. Being original can be incredibly difficult.

However, if you make your focus in an essay extremely narrow (as previously mentioned), you have a bit more room to work in. In a few thousand words, you aren't going to come up with a whole new theory. However, you might be able to make a small but meaningful difference within a narrow field. Try to narrow your focus in your next essay, in order to show some original thought.

9. Be confident.

Like originality, it's important to show confidence in your essays. After all, an essay is an argument, and the marker wants to see you get behind your ideas, rather than sit on the fence. You don't need to come across as foolhardy or blind to criticism, but don't be afraid to make strong claims if you have evidence to support them.

If you have space and time, try to address possible criticisms of your own argument. You can either address criticisms as you go, or devote a section towards the end of your essay on all the possible issues one might have with your ideas. Awareness of criticisms (as well as the ability to refute them) will show a level of sophistication that will put you far ahead of the competition.

10. Avoid lengthy introductions and conclusions.

Getting started on an essay is possibly the hardest part. Figuring out what you're going to say in the opening sentence can be a stumbling block, and it might be tempting just to start writing mindlessly. However, try to avoid this – you'll most likely ramble on, rather than getting to the point of your argument. Try to save introductions and conclusions for the very end of the writing stage of your essay. Once you know what you've said in the main body of your argument, you'll know what to write in the introduction and conclusion. This will help you to keep these sections laser-focused.

PLANNING AN ESSAY

The key to high grades in any assignment is planning. If you can nail a good plan and stick to it with all of your coursework, you can make sure that you cover all bases and increase your likelihood of excellence.

In a couple of pages you'll find a flowchart designed to take you through the step-by-step process of completing an assignment – from the earliest stage of choosing a topic to submitting it and receiving feedback. You might find that some of the steps do not apply to the type of assessment that you're working on. In that case, skip the step and move onto the next one.

Let's take a quick look at each of these steps:

Choose a Topic

This will only apply to you if you've been given a choice of topic to write your assignment about. Essay-based subjects usually have a list of different questions that you can choose from, but this may differ between universities, departments, and modules. If you aren't sure, check the department website, or ask your lecturer or seminar leader.

Other subjects may be more limited in the range of topics you can write your assignment on. If this is the case, you can ignore this step.

Choose and Dissect Exact Question

Once you've chosen a topic, or been given one, you might be given a choice of the exact question. It might be tempting to jump at the question on the topic you most enjoy, but be cautious of the questions themselves. While they might cover the topic that you think you understand really well, they might approach it from an angle that you aren't comfortable with. Carefully examine each question available to you before choosing one.

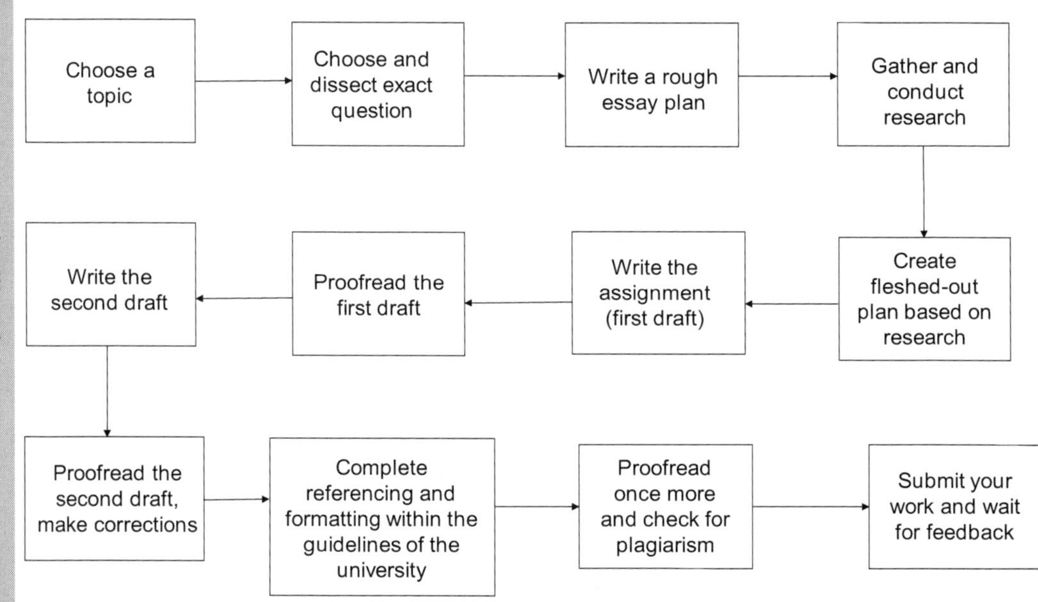
Choose a topic
Choose and dissect exact question
Write a rough essay plan
Gather and conduct research
Write the second draft
Proofread the first draft
Write the assignment (first draft)
Create fleshed-out plan based on research
Proofread the second draft, make corrections
Complete referencing and formatting within the guidelines of the university
Proofread once more and check for plagiarism
Submit your work and wait for feedback

After you've finished choosing a question, you need to take it apart and figure out what it's really asking of you. Keep an eye out for scope, both in terms of the scale of the area itself and how deep it expects you to go.

Write Rough Essay Plan

Once you've chosen your question and know what it's asking of you, it's time to start writing a rough plan. This won't be the final plan that you follow for the entire project – just a loose one to help you gather your thoughts for the research stage.

If you're writing an essay, try to construct a paragraph-by-paragraph plan in this stage. At the very least, you should have a good idea of what the sections of the essay or project are, and how they link together. Once you've finished doing this, you're ready to start the research phase of the essay-writing process!

Gather and Conduct Research

In this stage, you'll spend most of your time reading, working with others, or doing practical work so that you have something to support your assignment with. The exact nature of the research will depend on the subject and module that your assignment is in.

Create a Fleshed-Out Plan Based on Research

Once you've got all of your research together, you now need to apply it to your plan. If you're writing an essay, you want to look for anywhere in your plan where you've made some kind of claim. Add relevant evidence from your sources here, so that everything you're going to write in your essay is supported.

If you're doing some other kind of assignment, such as a write-up based on lab work, your entire piece will centre around your research. Again, include evidence from your own research to your plan where relevant, so your argument is well-supported.

To make things easier, try to make a note of all the page numbers and locations of everything you're citing in your work. This will save you from having to trawl through all your sources looking for the exact line and page where you got your evidence from.

Write the Assignment (First Draft)

Now that you've got a full and fleshed out plan, it's time to write the first draft. If you've taken your planning seriously, you shouldn't need to refer to any of your sources here – just follow each point of your plan, turning the bullet points and other short notes into full sentences.

If you've already made a full plan, this stage shouldn't take long at all. The key is to follow your plan as much as possible, and turn a series of notes into a coherent, eloquent piece of writing.

Proofread the First Draft

With a first draft finished, you should now read through it at least once. At this stage, keep an eye out for spelling, grammar, and punctuation errors – you don't want your work to contain any amateur mistakes.

Here, you can also get an idea of how your work flows from point to point. If you think some bits don't work properly, or something doesn't fit, make a note of it and then you can find a solution when you write the second draft.

Write the Second Draft

Writing the second draft is less a case of re-writing your whole assignment, and more of looking at the entire piece critically and trying to re-write parts so that they're even more concise. You might feel as though this is unnecessary, but going through and rewording things can help with clarity.

Proofread the Second Draft

As with the first draft, it's important to re-read your work to make sure there are no glaring errors.

Complete Referencing and Formatting

Hopefully, you've been referencing as you go along. If so, there should be little to do in this section when it comes to referencing. Just make sure that you've followed the referencing system that your university and department have specified, such as the Harvard Referencing System. You will probably also need to write a bibliography – do this at this stage.

In addition, you should make sure that the formatting of your work meets the specifications of the department. If your work is word-processed, they might specifically request certain fonts, font sizes, and line spacing. If relevant, check the guidelines set by your department since some universities will dock points from assignments that aren't formatted correctly.

Proofread and Check for Plagiarism

In this final stage, you want to proofread your work and specifically check for plagiarism. We'll discuss plagiarism in more detail later, but for now ensure that whenever you've used supporting evidence from a source, you've cited them properly. The aim of this is to make sure that you aren't passing off someone else's work as your own.

One way to check for plagiarism is to copy and paste sections of your own writing into a search engine. If this leads to results of places where you might have gathered ideas from, then you need to cite it as a source or remove the suspicious piece of text from your work. If you do remove it, make sure to replace it with your own work.

PROOFREADING

Proofreading is an essential part of the writing process for any kind of writing project. Whether you're solving Maths questions, writing an essay, or making a presentation, it's vital that you check for errors. When proofreading, you should look out for the following:

- Spelling, grammar, and punctuation errors;

- Inappropriate vocabulary;

- Unclear points;

- Messy paragraphs and sections;

- Sources without proper referencing;

- Factual errors.

Since this is a lot to keep an eye out for, you should probably do at least two proofreads of your work. On the first proofread, look out for the bigger issues, then move onto smaller errors such as typos in a later proofread, once you're happy with the content.

Another tip for proofreading is to wait for a little while after finishing a draft before reading it. If you start proofreading as soon as you've finished writing, you might be too burnt out to catch the issues. So, once you've finished writing your assignment, leave it for a couple of hours before taking a look at it. This way, you'll be looking at it with a 'fresh' pair of eyes, and you'll be more likely to spot things that need fixing.

Finally, if it's possible, have someone you trust take a look over your work. Even if they aren't an expert in the area you're writing on, they'll be able to tell you if there are spelling, grammar, and punctuation errors. Likewise, they'll probably be able to spot things which are unclear or messy. However, remember to be careful who you show your work to – someone might try to steal your ideas!

PLAGIARISM

Plagiarism is the act of taking someone else's work and, whether knowingly or unknowingly, try to pass it off as your own. This is an issue that is taken *extremely* seriously, and with good reason. For university students, punishments for plagiarism will vary depend on the severity of the case, but it isn't impossible for them to end in expulsion from the university. For this reason, it's vital that you avoid plagiarism in your work.

As previously mentioned, one of the best ways to avoid plagiarism is to make sure that you correctly cite any information as a source. Think of it this way: if you got the idea from somewhere else, then you need to make that clear in your work. This is why you should make note of everything that you're reading for your assignment – you'll have a record of everything you've learned, and where you got it from.

Of course, it's very unlikely that any idea that you've come up with is completely original. The chances are that, at some point, someone else has thought of the same thing, and they might have even published it. In these cases, you should make use of search engines to look up what you've written, and see if there are reputable sources which support it. If this is the case, then you should cite this source in your work as evidence.

REFERENCING

Referencing is an essential part of most assessed projects at school or university. In particular, students studying for essay-based subjects should train themselves to reference sources properly so that their work looks professional and so they also avoid accusations of plagiarism.

The type of referencing system that you'll have to use will differ depending on the university, course, and module that you're involved with. Some departments might be more relaxed about which referencing system you use, so long as you make sure that you are consistent. Your department should specify the referencing system that you need to use.

The following are some of the most prominent referencing systems in higher education, as well as (roughly) which subjects they apply to:

Referencing System	Format	Example
APA	Author (last name and initials). (Year of publication). *Title of book.* Place of publication: Publication.	Smith, J. (2013). *How to Reference.* London: How2become Ltd.
Chicago	Last name, First name. *Title of book.* Place of publication: Publisher, Year of publication.	Smith, John. *How to Reference.* London: How2become Ltd, 2013.
Harvard	Name of author(s) (last name and initials). (Year of publication). *Title of book.* Place of publication: Publisher.	Smith, J. (2013). *How to Reference.* London: How2become Ltd.
MLA	Last name, First name. *Title of book.* Publisher, Year of Publication.	Smith, John. *How to Reference.* How2become Ltd, 2013.
Vancouver	Name of authors(s) (last name and initials). *Title of book.* Place of publication: Publisher; Year of publication.	Smith, J. *How to Reference.* London: How2become Ltd; 2013.

Applicable Subjects	Notes
Social Sciences (e.g. Psychology or Sociology)	
History and Economics	
Arts and Humanities	Variant of the APA System
Arts and Humanities	
Medicine and Science	

Bear in mind that the examples above only demonstrate how to reference a book with a single author. Each referencing system has different formats for each type of work that you're referencing. On the next page, we've included some examples:

Edited books	Books with multiple authors	E-Books and pdf documents	Specific chapters of edited books
Newspaper articles	Online newspaper articles	Journals	Online journals
Websites	Blogs	Online publications	YouTube videos
Films	CDs	Lyrics	Religious texts
Acts of Parliament	Press releases	Interviews	Patent documents
Social media	Apps	Podcasts	Maps
Unpublished works	Video games	Archived documents	Annual reports

Each referencing system will have its own rules regarding each of these types of source. Before including one of these sources in your work, find out the exact format. It's also worth remembering that, when including citations in your work, you will need to cite sources as you go and include them in a bibliography.

The first of these is straightforward. Depending on the rules set by your referencing system, you will have to either cite sources *in-text* or by using *footnotes*.

Here's an example of an in-text citation in the Harvard referencing style:

Smith (2013, p. 135) notes that some universities prefer in-text citations.

This citation denotes the year that the book was published, as well as the exact page number it is referring to.

The alternative to the in-text method is to create a footnote. This is essentially the same as the in-text method, except the citation information appears at the bottom of the page:

In his book, Smith notes that other universities and referencing systems prefer the use of footnotes.[1]

---

1   Smith (2013), p. 136.

The footnotes system is sometimes preferable because it can prevent the text from becoming too cluttered. Most word-processing programs are capable of automating the footnoting system, making it easy to do.

Once you've cited all of your sources in text and written your assignment, you'll need to construct a bibliography. This is a summary of all of the works that you've used when writing your own assignment.

If you are at university, the contents of your bibliography will differ depending on your subject and department. Some prefer you to include everything that you've read regarding the topic of your assignment, even if you haven't referenced it in your work. Otherwise, they will ask you to only include works that you've referenced. Find out the conventions that your university has set before completing your bibliography.

Bibliographies should be filled out in alphabetical order by the surname of the author. So, 'Johnson, S.' would appear before 'Smith, J.'

A final tip for making referencing as easy as possible is to write a bibliography while you're gathering your research. This way, all you'll need to do is copy and paste the same bibliography into your assignment when you're finished with it. This is also a great method for keeping track of what you've read during the research stage, meaning you won't have to trawl back through your notes and books to find exact page numbers.

GETTING TOP MARKS

Now that we've taken a look at the assignment flowchart and touched on each area, let's look at some expert tips for each major stage of the assignment-writing process.

PLANNING YOUR COURSEWORK

In many ways, the planning stage of the assignment-writing process is the most important part of submitting an excellent piece of work. If you create a proper plan, then the bulk of the work you need to do will already be finished when you get to the main writing stage.

Treat the planning stage as though you were writing up the actual piece of work, but in a more condensed format. Try to create every point of your argument, with evidence and explanations, and put it inside your plan.

On top of this, divide these into paragraphs and sections, and make a note of ways in which each of them relates to the question and to the previous section. By doing this, you should create a plan that smoothly goes through every major point of your work. An essay or any other kind of written assignment which flows properly will have a much better chance of scoring high marks than one that feels clunky or disjointed.

As we've recommended, you should try to create two plans for your coursework. The first is a rough plan that outlines the general direction of your argument, as well as some basic points. Once you've done all of your research, you can adapt this plan to create a more fleshed-out one.

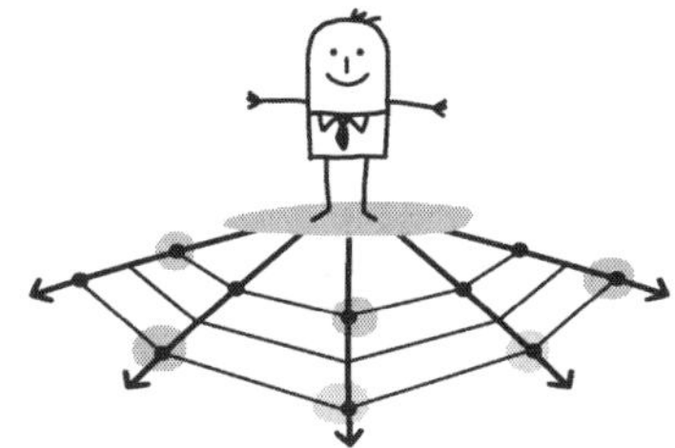

CONDUCTING RESEARCH

After planning, research is one of the most important parts of writing an assignment. No matter what course you're taking, if you fail to provide evidence for your argument, then you will get very few marks. Without conducting thorough research, you won't have the evidence you need in order to create a high-quality piece of work.

A lot of the tips we suggested about how to work independently are relevant here. In particular, try to do the following when it comes to gathering information for your coursework:

1. If you're at university then start by using recommended reading lists provided by the department. This will be a curated list of sources which are relevant to your topic. In addition, they *should* be books, journals, and other types of sources which are suited to your level of study.

2. Make use of *reputable* online sources alongside books. By 'reputable', we mean journals and other works that have been formally published/peer reviewed.

3. Unless specified otherwise, try not to use amateur blog posts or online encyclopaedias.

When it comes to university research, you should have a wider range of resources available:

The first port of call should be your university library. Try to get hold of the most essential books from the recommended reading list as soon as possible, since these are the most likely to be taken out by someone else. Once you've got these, read the relevant chapters and take notes on anything that might be useful to your assignment, as well as the page numbers. Get all of the information you need as soon as possible, just in case the book gets recalled and you have to return it.

If you've exhausted all of the relevant materials in the library, get yourself online and see what you can access there. Quite often, universities will give you login details for online journals and journal search engines, giving you access to a wealth of articles and other material that might be useful for your work. Be sure to reference these correctly, since they must be cited in a slightly different way to print journals.

If you don't have access to any of these, some of the sources you need might be accessible in other places. In particular, extremely old works such as Ancient Greek philosophical texts can often be found in their entirety online and free of charge. Of course, more recent works will not be available in this way for copyright reasons.

If this doesn't cover everything, try and find some students on your course in the years above you. If you're lucky, they might have a copy of the book that you need that they could lend to you. If your university has a mentoring network set up between students across years, then this might be a great opportunity to get hold of key materials.

If there are still resources that you need after taking these steps, then you might have to buy the books yourself. When doing this, make sure you buy the correct edition of the book, since different publications of the same book might not be quite as relevant. This is especially the case for translated works, where there might be a large disparity between two separate translations. Reading lists set by departments and modules should include the exact versions you need if this is the case.

Once you have all of the sources you need, it's time to get reading and note-making. When it comes to coursework, it's often better to write out the key information in exact quotes. This is so that you don't exactly re-word something in a way which changes the meaning of the sentence. While you should almost always paraphrase rather than quote directly when writing your assignment, re-writing the quote in full at this stage is preferable. Remember to keep track of page numbers so that referencing is easier later on.

Although most research that students conduct involves reading and taking notes from articles, some courses might require lab work for assignments. In these cases, the work you will need to complete will be set out for you, and you'll likely be given a slot of time to do the lab work. Once you've finished it, you'll probably need to write a report on it. The tips in this chapter will apply to writing a lab report, but be sure to consult documents from your department which might specify conventions and formatting styles.

Once you've gathered all of the research you need, we strongly suggest adding the relevant information to your plan, fleshing it out even more. You might find that the plan you wrote before doesn't quite work in light of what you've learned from research. This isn't a problem: re-write your plan until it suits the kind of argument you want to make.

WRITING YOUR ASSIGNMENT

Once you've finished planning and researching, it's time to write your piece of work. If you've planned well, this shouldn't be too difficult a task; all you're really doing is turning short bullet points into full sentences. However, there are some tips you can take on board to improve your chances of getting the top grades.

Write the Introduction and Conclusion Last

Sometimes, figuring out a great introduction can be difficult. You want to avoid opening with grandiose, sweeping statements, but you also want to give a general idea of what your argument is. If you've planned properly, you should already know the shape and direction of your argument. However, it's usually better to jump straight into the main body of work. Then, you can write a fully focused and sharp introduction.

Once you've finished writing everything, then you can head back and write a great introduction and conclusion based on what's in the main part of your assignment.

Keep Things Simple

You might be aware of the famous adage from *Hamlet* which states that 'brevity is the soul of wit'. In other words, you should not waste the reader's time; explain points properly, but in as few words as necessary.

In addition, you don't always need to use overly complicated terminology. In some cases, you'll have no choice but to, but in many cases simpler language is preferable. In some subjects, you might be marked specifically on the wealth of your vocabulary and your grasp on language. In these cases, you can be more decadent with your terms.

Another way to keep things simple is to use shorter sentences. The longer a sentence is, the more unwieldy it can become. In turn, this might lead to run-on sentences which are more difficult to read than shorter sentences. Experiment with the length of your sentences to see if making them shorter gives your work more clarity.

CREATIVE WRITING

Of course, writing isn't all about aloof academic discourse or thorough technical analysis. Whether it's for school, university, or for the love of it, you may prefer to write creatively. While 'rules' on the art of writing poems, short stories, or novels may be difficult or even impossible to pin down, there is some general advice you can follow to help you get ideas flowing, and to get the best out of these ideas. Let's cover some questions you should ask yourself before embarking on your creative journey.

1. **Why are you writing?**

    Before you set about doing any writing, it's important to gain a clear understanding of what's motivating you to do so. Are you writing to learn more about yourself or others? Are you critiquing anything in particular? Do you just have a really good idea for a story? There is no 'right' answer to the question of 'Why are you writing?' but make sure that you have one. Clear aims and objectives will serve to focus all of your future travails, and keep you motivated throughout the process.

2. **Who is your intended audience?**

As well as the question above, you should ascertain who it is you're writing for – who do you expect will get the most from your writing? Again, the answer to this could be you, which is fine. However, if you plan on sharing your work (which you should!) you need to consider some demographics. Are you writing for children or young adults? Are you aiming to resonate with certain genders? Or even: are you aiming to fulfil the conventions of a particular genre? Of course, not knowing this from the outset could mean that your work may end up without direction, or even a point. Planning in this way will also make writing a lot easier – you'll be able to maintain a clear focus.

3. **How much time are you willing to commit?**

Of course, planning in general is an extremely important part of any writing project. High up on your list of priorities on this matter should be setting a realistic work timetable. How many hours per week are you willing or able to spend writing? Once decided, you need to stick to your plan and make sure you spend the hours you have committed to the project writing, reading, and editing. This will help you see your project out and avoid creative stasis.

4. **How much are you reading?**

It is often said that the best writers are also the most avid readers. So, you should spend as much time as possible reading! Read everything – novels, works of non-fiction, plays and poems. In doing so, you will find inspiration and with it motivation to write. Also, you'll gain a deeper understanding of style and voice, which will help you cultivate your own as you come across a wider range of other voices. Having said this, it can be difficult to balance writing and reading time – you don't want to risk burning yourself out reading. Experiment with the amount of time you spend reading and writing to find your most productive balance.

5. **Do you have an accurate view of your own work?**

This is a question you want to ask yourself throughout your writing process. In finding the answer, you'll have to consider whether you are distant enough from your work to critique it effectively. While this sounds odd, it can be quite easy to become too close to your work – meaning you become blind to its flaws and strengths alike. Train yourself to read through your work as if it was someone else's, and you'll be much better placed to assess and improve it.

WANT TO LEARN EVEN MORE REVISION TRICKS?

CHECK OUT OUR OTHER REVISION GUIDES:

ACHIEVE 100% SERIES

FOR MORE INFORMATION ON OUR REVISION GUIDES, PLEASE CHECK OUT THE FOLLOWING:

WWW.HOW2BECOME.COM

RAPID STUDY SKILLS FOR STUDENTS

Get Access To

FREE Psychometric

Tests

www.PsychometricTestsOnline.co.uk

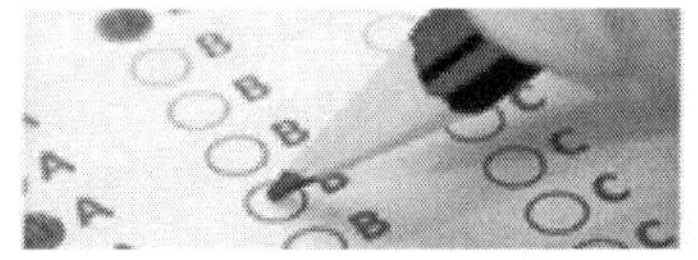

Printed and bound by CPI Group (UK) Ltd, Croydon, CR0 4YY

06/07/2026

02157570-0001